Germán Castro Bernal

Incoterms 2020

Germán Castro Bernal

Incoterms 2020

Practical Guide to International Trade Operations

ScienciaScripts

Imprint
Any brand names and product names mentioned in this book are subject to trademark, brand or patent protection and are trademarks or registered trademarks of their respective holders. The use of brand names, product names, common names, trade names, product descriptions etc. even without a particular marking in this work is in no way to be construed to mean that such names may be regarded as unrestricted in respect of trademark and brand protection legislation and could thus be used by anyone.

Cover image: www.ingimage.com

This book is a translation from the original published under ISBN 978-620-0-39761-4.

Publisher:
Sciencia Scripts
is a trademark of
Dodo Books Indian Ocean Ltd., member of the OmniScriptum S.R.L Publishing group
str. A.Russo 15, of. 61, Chisinau-2068, Republic of Moldova Europe
Printed at: see last page
ISBN: 978-620-0-93448-2

INCOTERMS® 2020

PRACTICAL GUIDE FOR INTERNATIONAL TRADE OPERATIONS

GERMAN CASTRO BERNAL

All you need to know about Incoterms® 2020

Incoterms are the International Commercial Terms, from the English International Commercial Terms, which compressed is INCOTERMS. These terms are developed by the International Chamber of Commerce (ICC) based on the practice of traders and merchants around the world, seeking to homogenize their contracts, published in 1936 the first edition of the Incoterms rules.

In the last decades there has always been a revision of the Incoterms rules coinciding with the first year of each one of them: 1990, 2000, 2010. The latest version is the Incoterms 2020.

Incoterms seek to facilitate the operation of international trade transactions and establish a set of terms and rules that determine the rights and obligations of both the seller and the buyer:

☐ Where the delivery of the goods takes place.

☐ Who assumes the risks of that purchase and how far.

☐ By what means of transport the goods will travel.

☐ Whether or not there is an obligation to insure the operation and who will be responsible.

Incoterms 2020:

In the latest version 2020, 11 terms are maintained, however, the term DAT (Delivered at Terminal) has been replaced by the term DPU (Delivered at Place Unloaded).

The ICC has classified the Incoterms according to the mode of transport used. Thus, the first group includes 7 Incoterms (EXW, FCA, CPT, CIP, DAP, DPU and DDP) that can be used regardless of the mode of transport and whether they use multimodal transport. The second group includes 4 Incoterms (FAS, FOB, CFR and CIF) to be used when the goods are transported by sea.

It should be noted that the first letter of the abbreviation provides information on the approach to that group of terms:

- **Terms beginning with the letter E (EXW)** indicate **that** the seller's responsibilities are met when the products are available for shipment by the carrier chosen by the buyer.
- **Terms beginning with the letter F (FCA, FAS and FOB)** refer to shipments where the seller does not pay the principal cost of the shipment or the principal carriage.
- **Terms beginning with the letter C (CFR, CPT, CIF and CIF)** refer to shipments in which the seller pays a portion of the shipment, usually the transportation at origin and the main transportation, but the seller's responsibility ends when the products are delivered to the carrier somewhere on the seller's side.

- **Terms beginning with the letter D (DAP, DPU and DDP)** are terms of delivery at destination because the seller delivers somewhere in the buyer's country. The shipper's or seller's responsibility ends when the goods reach a predefined point. Under these terms, the seller pays for pre-carriage, main carriage and carriage afterwards.

Incoterms 2020 changes.

While the number of Incoterms remains the same, there are some changes:

☐ **New term Incoterms DPU (Delivered Placed Unloaded), which replaces DAT (Delivered at Terminal)**
This change of acronym is a simple renaming as the duties and functions of both terms are exactly the same. The change of name is justified because the goods can be unloaded not only at a terminal (port, airport, quay, container station or road terminal, etc.) but also at any other agreed point in the country of destination that has equipment to unload the goods from the means of transport, such as a factory or warehouse.

☐ **Changes in the insurance terms Incoterms CIP and CIF**

In the Incoterms CIP term, the seller is obliged to take out transport insurance on behalf of the buyer with comprehensive coverage, which corresponds to Clause A of the Institute Cargo Clauses in London (IUA/LMA). However, if both parties agree, they may agree to take out insurance offering lesser coverage (Clause C of the Institute Cargo Clauses). In contrast, for the Incoterms CIF term the seller is only obliged to take out insurance with minimum coverage, which corresponds to Clause C of the Institute Cargo Clauses of London (IUA/LMA). Similarly, in CIF if both parties agree, they can agree to take out an insurance that offers more coverage (Clause A of the Institute Cargo Clauses).

☐ **Changes in the detail of the term Incoterms FCA**

The Incoterms 2020 version provides the option, in case of sea transport, for the buyer to instruct the carrier (shipping line or its agent) he has contracted to issue a Bill of Lading (B/L) in the name of the seller with the notation "on board", which indicates that the goods have been loaded on board the ship. This is the most common transport document used in the operation of letters of credit to justify the delivery of the goods and thus make payment to the seller.

Importance of Incoterms rules:

Incoterms rules are very useful because they simplify international contracting with only 3 letters and a place where the goods are delivered, saving pages of buyer and seller obligations, and avoiding doubts and complications.

A great advantage of Incoterms is that they mean the same in all countries, even in the United States, as the Uniform Commercial Code (UCC) existed until 2007.

However, we should not be confused, since with all the Incoterms do not replace the contract of sale only specify it in key aspects.

The transfer of ownership is not decided in the Incoterms used but in the applicable law of the transaction. For example, in some legal systems such as French or English law a title or document is sufficient to transfer ownership, in others such as Spanish law a title and mode is required, i.e. it is not sufficient to have a justification of ownership, but possession of the property is also required.

In conclusion, the Incoterms rules are international, global, commercial uses codified by the International Chamber of Commerce.

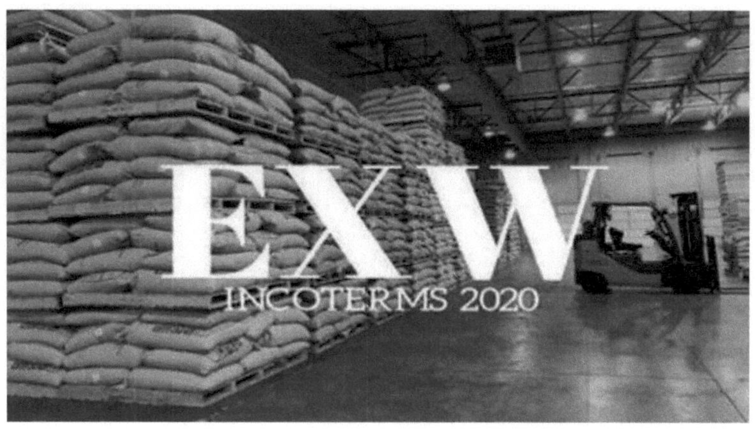

The term EXW stands for "*Ex* Works". In a sale and purchase operation under the EXW term, the seller delivers the goods when he has them at the disposal of the buyer, outside the seller's premises, or in another agreed place (workshop, factory, warehouse, etc.); without dispatching them for export or loading them onto a transport vehicle.

EXW represents the minimum obligation for the selling company. Therefore, this term is recommended for domestic transactions.

Incoterms EXW features:

- **Type of transport:** Any means of transport, including multimodal (containers)
- **Place of delivery:** At the seller's premises (factory, warehouse, workshop, etc.)

- **Situation of the goods (loading/unloading):** Duly packed and checked, ready to be loaded on the first means of transport (usually truck).
- **Delivery document:** Collection document from the first carrier or equivalent documents.
- **Type of cargo:** Any type of cargo, except bulk and large loads.
- **Hiring of the main transport:** Buyer.
- **Taking out transport insurance:** There is no obligation for either party. However, it is advisable for the buyer to take out insurance, since he is the one who assumes the risk in international transport.
- **Transfer of risk from the seller to the buyer:** At the time of delivery, before the goods are loaded on the first means of transport, at the seller's

premises.

- □ **Pre-shipment inspection:** Buyer.

- □ **Export clearance:** Buyer.

- □ **Import clearance:** Buyer.

- □ **Means of payment to be used:** Simple (transfer, payment order, check, etc.)

Incoterms EXW obligations of the parties.
Seller:

- □ Notify the buyer that the goods are ready to be picked up

- □ Assume the cost of verification, quality control, measurement, weighing, counting, packaging of products, marking, among others, until the goods are properly conditioned so that they can begin international transit.
- □ To deliver the goods within the agreed time, the seller is not obliged to load the goods on any collecting vehicle or means of transport.
    - □ Provide a commercial invoice and packing list, or an equivalent electronic document, and generate evidence of conformity or proof of delivery
    - □ Provide additional or complementary local documentation for the export of the goods [when necessary]

Buyer:

- □ Go or send your consignee to pick up the goods at the agreed time.

- □ Verify the goods, and assume all costs and risks of the international traffic of the goods that are generated since the collection.
- □ Receive the goods in conformity when they are delivered.

- □ Pay the price of the goods as agreed.

Incoterms EXW cost and risk:

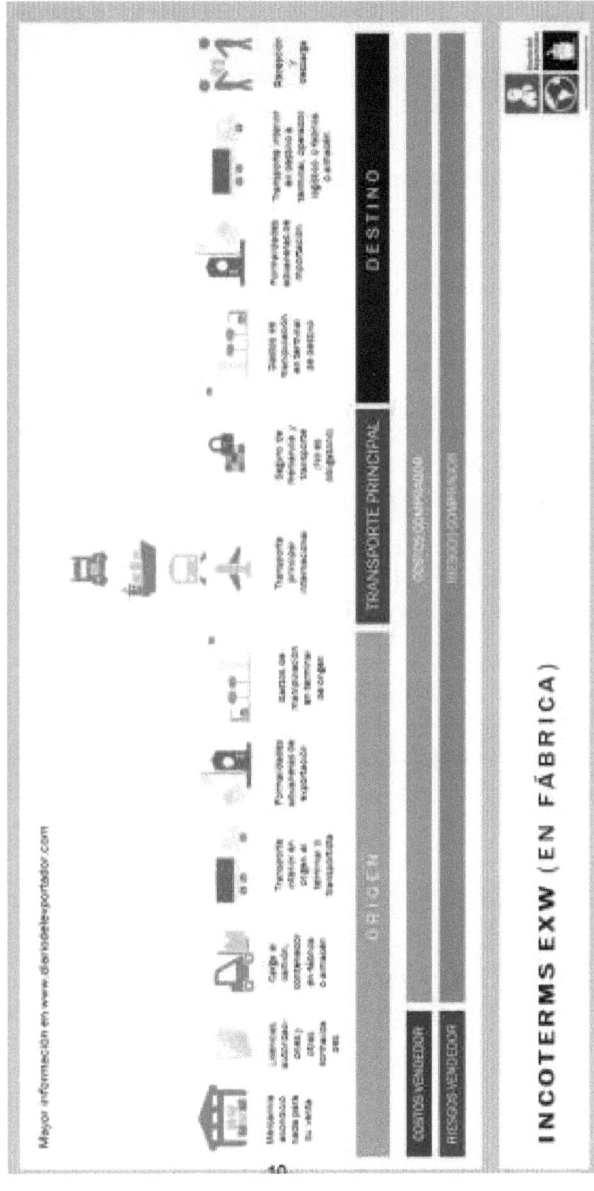

The term Incoterms in the contract:

Since the transfer of risk and distribution of logistics and customs costs is dependent on the place of delivery, it is essential to specify the place of delivery of the goods as clearly as possible in the contract and pro forma invoice. The International Chamber of Commerce recommends the following structure: **The term Incoterms + place of delivery + Incoterms 2020 Rule**

Example: EXW, Nestor Gambeta Avenue 2875, Callao, Lima, Peru, Incoterms 2020 Rules

Notes and recommendations:

The International Chamber of Commerce advises the term EXW for national transactions and, FCA for international trade, except in conditions of maximum confidence, both from the seller's point of view, because he loses control of the goods and the guarantees that the export formalities are carried out correctly, and from the buyer's point of view, because he has to bear all the costs, from the very collection and loading in the country of origin, and all the documentary and customs formalities.

If the seller wants the least possible responsibility in the operation, or the buyer wants to control it as much as possible, we recommend that, at least, the operation is carried out in FCA conditions, Free Carrier or Designated Place, in this case: the seller's warehouse.

As we will see in the following FCA Incoterms, the main difference is that the seller is responsible for loading the goods on the means that the buyer puts for that purpose, (avoiding that outside personnel handle the goods within the facility) as well as the customs export procedures, which guarantees you have an official document that justifies having issued an invoice exempt from VAT for subsequent collection-deduction.

The term FCA stands for "Free Carrier". In a sales transaction under the FCA term, the seller delivers the goods to the carrier designated by the buyer at the seller's premises or another designated place. The seller is obliged to clear the goods for export.

The term FCA is used instead of EWX when the seller is in a better position to load the goods and when documentation is required for tax purposes. Then EXW for local sales and FCA for international sales.

Incoterms FCA features:

- **Type of transport:** Any means of transport, including multimodal (containers)

- **Place of delivery:** At the seller's premises (factory, warehouse, workshop, etc.); or At different points in the seller's country (transport terminals, airport, etc.)

- **Status of goods (loading/unloading):** Loaded on **the** first transport (usually truck) designated by the buyer; or ready for unloading at the place of delivery.

- **Delivery document:** Collection document from the first carrier or equivalent document; or Delivery document from the seller's carrier to the international carrier designated by the buyer.

- **Type of cargo:** Any type of cargo (general, complete and groupage).

  - **Hiring of the main transport:** Buyer.

  - **Taking out transport insurance:** There is no obligation for either party. However, it is advisable for the buyer to take out insurance, since he is the one who assumes the risk in international transport.

- **Transfer of risk from the seller to the buyer:** Once the goods have been loaded onto the transport designated by the buyer, at the seller's own facilities; or At the place of delivery, before the goods are unloaded for delivery to the carrier designated by the buyer.
- **Pre-shipment inspection:** Buyer, unless required by the seller's country in which case it will be at the seller's expense.
- **Export clearance:** Seller.
- **Import clearance:** Buyer.
- Means of payment to be used: **Simple (transfer, payment order, check, etc.), as documentary (letter of credit, documentary collection, etc.)**

Incoterms FCA obligations of the parties.

Salesman:

- Notify the buyer when the goods are ready to be picked up at the agreed place.
- Deliver the goods to the carrier or to the consignee designated by the buyer, at the agreed place of delivery, if there is no agreed place, then the seller can determine the best location.
- Pay all costs until the goods have been placed in the agreed place, including those generated by customs clearance at origin.
- Generate evidence of conformity or proof of delivery of the goods and assist the buyer in obtaining the corresponding transport document or its receipt.
- Provide a commercial invoice and packing list or equivalent electronic document.
- To assist the buyer, ensuring the availability of services, information and complementary or additional documentation for the international traffic of goods.

Buyer:

- □ Provide sufficient information to the seller about the carrier and the transfer or shipment of the cargo.
- □ Verify and receive the goods in conformity, within the time and in the place agreed.
- □ Assume all costs and risks of the international traffic of the goods that are generated since they are received by the carrier, including those additional that could be generated during delivery.
- □ To receive the documents or receipts in conformity.
- □ Pay the price of the goods as agreed.
- □ Pay for additional services or documents requested from the seller.

Incoterms FCA costs and risks:

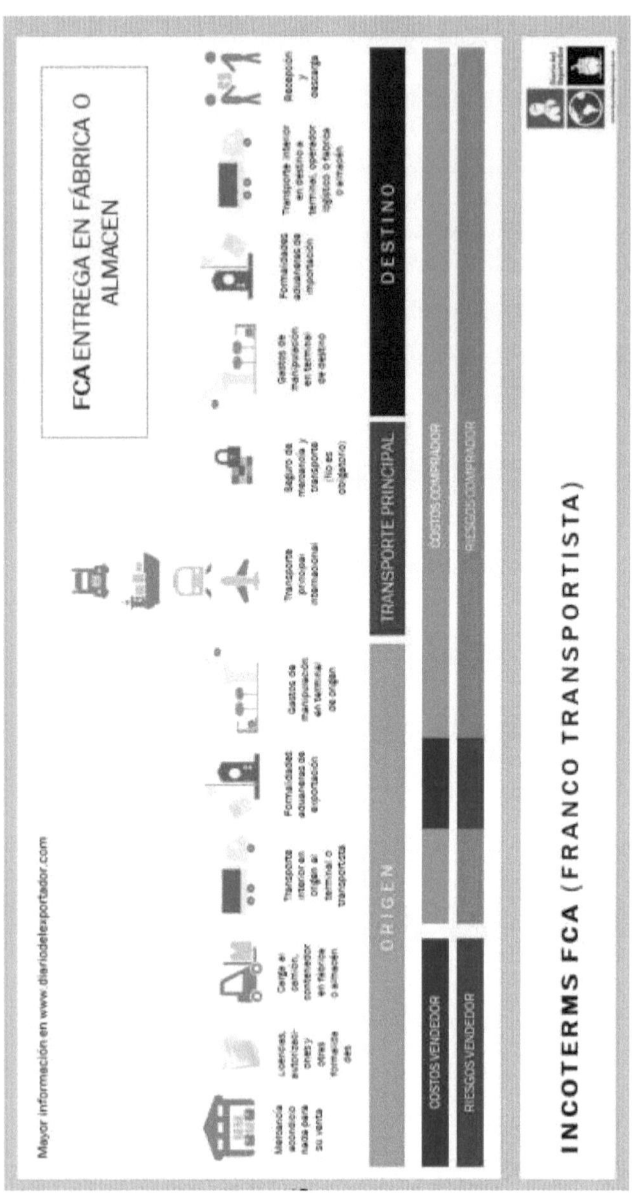

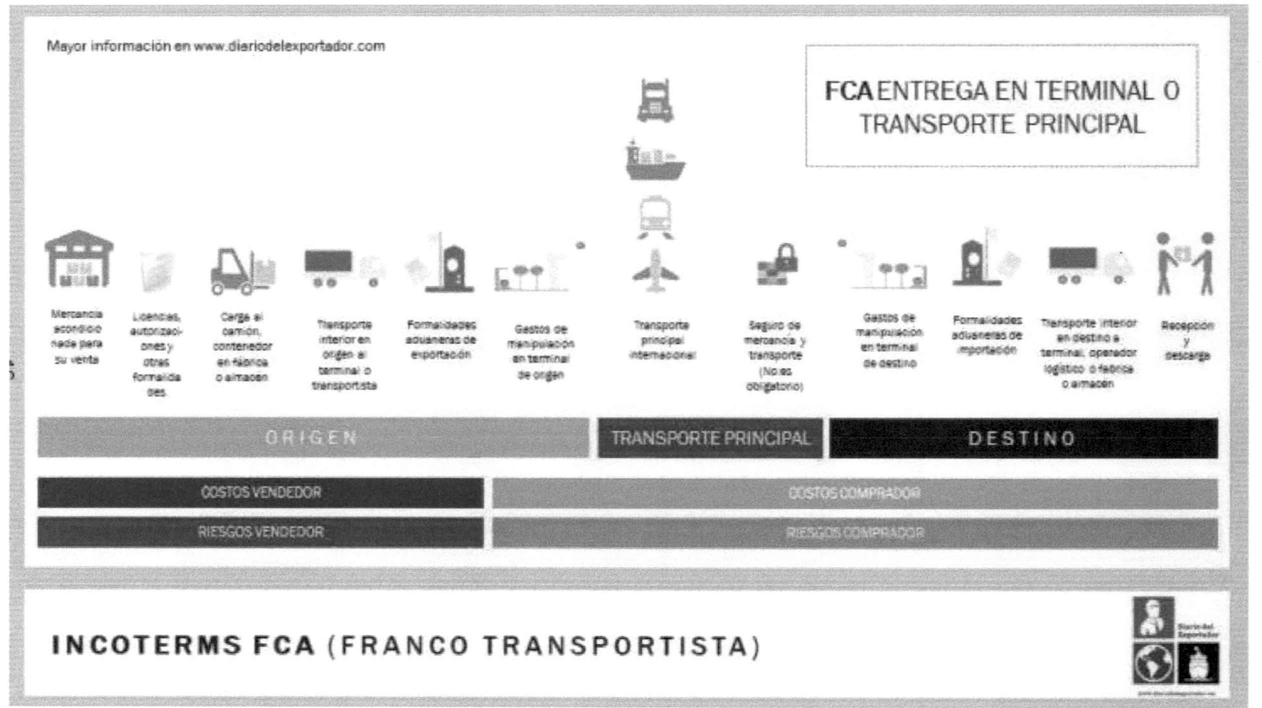

INCOTERMS FCA (FRANCO TRANSPORTISTA)

FCA Incoterms in the contract:

Since the transfer of risk and distribution of logistics and customs costs is dependent on the place of delivery, it is essential to specify the place of delivery of the goods as clearly as possible in the contract and pro forma invoice. The International Chamber of Commerce recommends the following structure: **The term Incoterms + place of delivery + Incoterms 2020 Rule.**

Notes and recommendations:

From our point of view, FCA, Free Carrier is the Incoterms term that should substitute the so used FOB for shipments of merchandise in container, since, in this way, the seller avoids the costs of port handling and shipping that are not controllable by him, since they are contracted by the buyer.

Despite having some control over shipments, with FCA we still do not have a guarantee that the goods will end up in the country to which we have sold them, and having little management responsibility compared to the buyer, we have few negotiating elements other than the goods themselves.

Therefore we recommend that, FCA Port of Loading is the minimum Incoterms to be used, being in most cases more beneficial for the selling company to manage the transport to at least the port of destination - CPT/CIP in multimodal and CIF/CFR if it is only by sea.

Change in ACF 2020:

When the negotiated form of payment is made by means of a letter of credit, banks most often require the presentation of an "on board" shipping document. In FCA, since the delivery of the goods from the seller to the buyer is made before the contracting of the main transport and this is in charge of the buyer, the seller has no possibility to get the mentioned document of shipment.

To address this situation, the INCOTERMS 2020 offer the possibility for the buyer and seller to agree that the buyer will instruct the carrier to deliver a shipping document "on board" to the seller. Even so, our recommendation is to avoid letters of credit with FCA or FOB shipments and, if there is no other option, get the issuing bank to replace the maritime shipping document with any document that, without waiting for the goods to be shipped at origin, certifies that the seller has fulfilled its delivery obligation to the buyer.

Otherwise, everything we have gained in terms of avoiding risks that we do not control within a port or costs that vary greatly depending on the shipping line or agent handling the main transport, as well as complying with the agreed delivery, we will have lost if we continue to depend on receiving a copy of the shipping document "on board" that is not delivered until the vessel has left the port of origin in order to comply with the terms of the letter of credit.

The term FAS stands for "Free Alongside Ship". In a sales transaction under the FAS term the seller delivers the goods alongside the ship designated by the buyer (for example, on the quay or on a barge) at the designated port of shipment. The seller transfers the risk and assumes all costs up to the point of loading at the named port of shipment, as well as costs related to export clearance.

Incoterms FAS features:

- **Type of transport:** Exclusively for sea transport. Not recommended for multimodal transport (containers).

- **Place of delivery:** alongside the ship (on the quay or on a barge) at the port of embarkation.

- Status of goods (loading/unloading): Ready to be loaded on the vessel designated by the buyer.

- **Delivery document:** Dock receipt or shipping receipt.

- **Type of cargo:** Bulk, large loads and complex cargo (machinery).

- **Hiring of the main transport:** Buyer.

- **Taking out transport insurance:** There is no obligation for either party. However, it is advisable for the buyer to take out insurance, since he is the one who assumes the risk in international transport.

- **Transfer of risk from seller to buyer:** Once the goods have been made available to the buyer at the quay or loading point in the port designated by the buyer.

- **Pre-shipment inspection:** Buyer, unless required by the seller's country in which case it will be at the seller's expense.

- **Export clearance:** Seller.

- **Import clearance:** Buyer.

- **Means of payment to be used:** Simple (transfer, payment order, check, etc.), as documentary (letter of credit, documentary collection, etc.)

Incoterms FAS obligations of the parties.

Salesman:

- Notify the buyer that the goods have been placed next to the ship

- Place the goods next to the vessel at the agreed-upon port of shipment, within the agreed-upon time frame.

- Pay all costs of delivery of the goods until they are placed next to the ship, including those generated by customs clearance in the country of origin.
- Provide a commercial invoice and packing list or equivalent electronic document, and generate evidence of conformity or proof of delivery.
- To assist the buyer, ensuring the availability of services, information and complementary or additional documentation for the international traffic of goods.

Buyer:
- Provide sufficient information to the seller about the vessel, the ship's itinerary and the port of shipment.
- Receive the goods in conformity at the agreed place and time.

- Assume all costs and risks of the international traffic of the goods that are generated since they are placed next to the designated vessel.
- Pay the price of the goods as agreed.

- Pay for additional services or documents requested from the seller.

Incoterms FAS costs and risks:

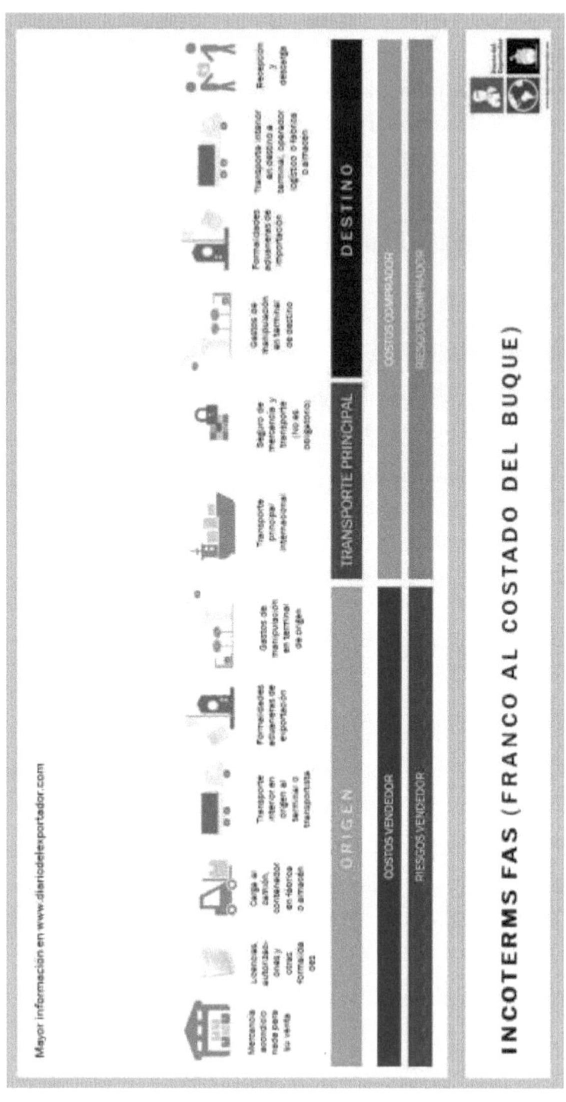

FAS Incoterms in the contract

Since the transfer of risk and distribution of logistics and customs costs is dependent on the place of delivery, it is essential to specify the place of delivery of the goods as clearly as possible in the contract and pro forma invoice. The International Chamber of Commerce recommends the following structure: **The term Incoterms + place of delivery + Incoterms 2020 Rule**

Example: FAS, Paita, Piura, Peru Incoterms 2020 rules

Notes and recommendations:

This is a good option if the contracts of maritime charter are not well controlled, since it forces us to clear customs, as well as limiting the possibility of unforeseen costs, by having to manage the transport from our warehouse to the terminal, and the export customs clearance, leaving the rest of the expenses and management on behalf of the buyer.

This term should be used exclusively when it comes to sea or inland waterway transport. It is not used for transport by container (where FCA must be used). It is usually used in the transport of bulk goods such as coal, molasses, metal waste, etc, which are transported in the hold of a ship, or special goods which, due to their nature and dimensions, require a very special ship loading operation such as wind turbines, buses, etc.

The term FOB stands for "Free On Board". In a sales transaction under the FOB term the seller delivers the goods on board the ship designated by the buyer at the designated port of shipment. The seller transfers the risk and assumes all costs until the goods are on board the ship, as well as the costs related to export clearance.

FOB Incoterms features:

- **Type of transport:** Exclusively for sea transport. Not recommended for multimodal transport (containers).
- **Place of delivery:** On board the vessel at the port of shipment designated by the buyer.
- **Location of the goods (loading/unloading):** On board the vessel designated by the buyer.
- **Delivery document:** Bill of Lading (B/L) or shipping receipt.
- **Type of cargo:** Bulk, large loads and complex cargo (machinery)
- **Hiring of the main transport:** Buyer.
- **Taking out transport insurance:** There is no obligation for either party. However, it is advisable for the buyer to take out insurance, since he is the one who assumes the risk in international transport.
- **Transfer of risk from the seller to the buyer:** Once the goods have been placed on board the ship, in the port designated by the buyer.
- **Pre-shipment inspection:** Buyer, unless required by the seller's country in which case it will be at the seller's expense.

☐ **Export clearance:** Seller.

☐ **Import clearance:** Buyer.

☐ **Means of payment to be used:** Simple (transfer, payment order, check, etc.), as documentary (letter of credit, documentary collection, etc.)

Incoterms FOB obligations of the parties.

Salesman:
☐ Notify the delivery of the goods on board the agreed vessel.

☐ Deliver the goods on board the agreed vessel.

☐ Pay all costs until the cargo has been placed on the vessel that will move it to its destination, including those generated by customs clearance in the country of origin.

☐ Generate evidence of conformity or proof of delivery of the goods and assist the buyer in obtaining the corresponding transport document or its receipt.

☐ Provide a commercial invoice and packing list, or an equivalent electronic document

☐ To assist the buyer, ensuring the availability of services, information and complementary or additional documentation for the international traffic of goods.

Buyer:
☐ Provide sufficient information to the seller to perform the transfer or shipment of the cargo.
☐ Receive the goods in conformity, after they have been loaded on the ship.
☐ Assume all costs and risks of the international traffic of the goods generated since they are loaded on the ship.
☐ To receive the documents or receipts in conformity.

☐ Pay the price of the goods as agreed.

☐ Pay for additional services or documents requested from the seller.

Incoterms FOB costs and risks:

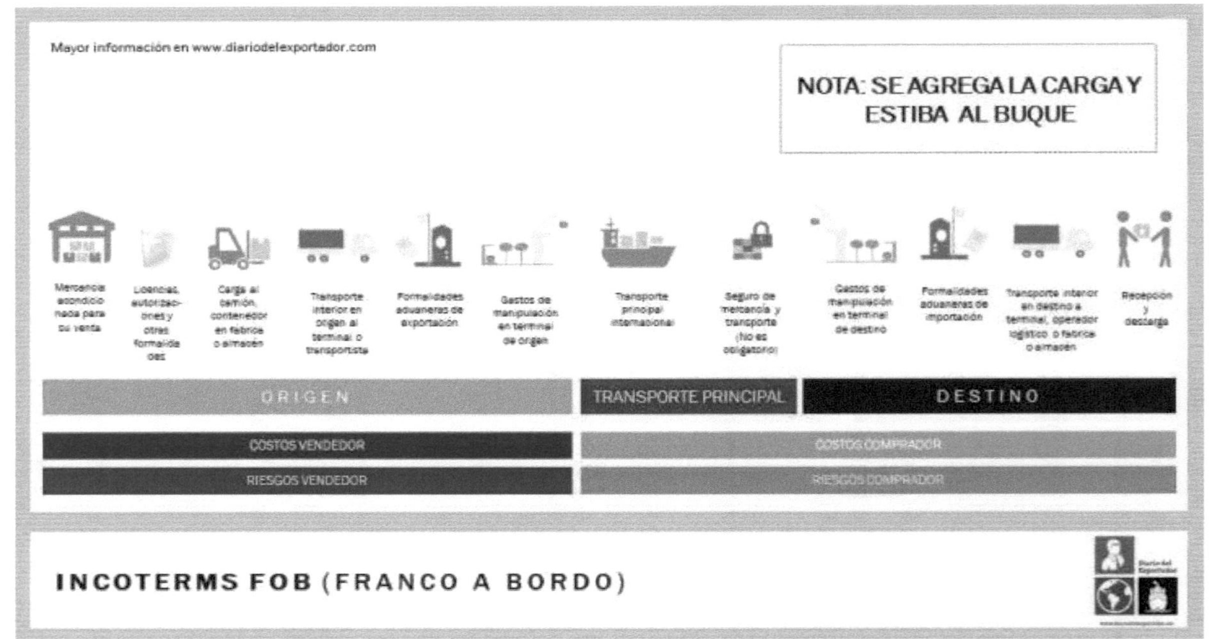

Mayor información en www.diariodelexportador.com
NOTA: SE AGREGA LA CARGA Y ESTIBA AL BUQUE
Mercancía acondicionada para su venta
Licencias, autorizaciones y otras formalidades
Carga al camión, contenedor en fábrica o almacén
Transporte interior en origen al terminal o transportista
Formalidades aduaneras de exportación
Gastos de manipulación en terminal de origen
Transporte principal internacional
Seguro de mercancía y transporte (no es obligatorio)
Gastos de manipulación en terminal de destino
Formalidades aduaneras de importación
Transporte interior en destino a terminal, operador logístico o fábrica o almacén
Recepción y descarga
ORIGEN
TRANSPORTE PRINCIPAL
DESTINO
COSTOS VENDEDOR
COSTOS COMPRADOR
RIESGOS VENDEDOR
RIESGOS COMPRADOR
INCOTERMS FOB (FRANCO A BORDO)
Diario del Exportador

FOB Incoterms in the contract:

Since the transfer of risk and distribution of logistics and customs costs is dependent on the place of delivery, it is essential to specify the place of delivery of the goods as clearly as possible in the contract and pro forma invoice. The International Chamber of Commerce recommends the following structure: **The term Incoterms + place of delivery + Incoterms 2020 Rule**

Example: FOB, Matarani, Arequipa, Peru Incoterms 2020 rules

Notes and recommendations:

FOB is a good option in maritime transport, if the contracts of maritime charter are not well controlled, since it forces us to clear customs, although it forces us to assume port handling costs that we may not know at the time of signing the contract.

When not to use FOB? When we may have difficulties in obtaining a B/L (Bill of Lading) which is a necessary document when the means of payment is a documentary credit.

If the goods are in containers, it is customary for the exporter to place the goods in the possession of the carrier at a terminal and not at the side of the vessel. Therefore, Incoterms FOB would be inappropriate and Incoterms FCA should be used, thus avoiding difficulties with documentation and having more control over costs.

The term CPT stands for "Carriage Paid To. In a sales transaction under the CPT term, the seller contracts and pays the costs of transportation needed to bring the goods to the designated place of destination, as well as the costs related to export clearance. The risks of loss and damage pass to the buyer from the moment the goods are delivered to the carrier's custody.

In the term CPT the risk is transferred and the costs are transferred in different places. It is therefore important that the seller and the buyer clearly specify both the place of delivery, where the risk is transferred to the buyer, and the designated place of destination to which the seller must contract for transport.

CPT Incoterms features.

- **Type of transport:** Any means of transport, including multimodal (containers)
- **Place of delivery:** At the point where the goods are delivered to the first carrier contracted by the seller
- **Location of the goods (loading/unloading):** Loaded on the first means of transport contracted by the seller.
- **Delivery document:** Shipment document (CRM, CIM, B/L or AWB)
- **Type of cargo:** Any type of cargo (general, complete and groupage).
- **Hiring of the main transport:** Seller.
- **Taking out transport insurance:** There is no obligation for either party. However, it is advisable for the buyer to take out insurance, since he is the one who assumes the risk in international transport.

- **Transfer of risk from seller to buyer:** When the goods are delivered to the first carrier contracted by the seller.
- **Pre-shipment inspection:** Buyer, unless required by the seller's country in which case it will be at the seller's expense.
- **Export clearance:** Seller.
- **Import clearance:** Buyer.
- **Means of payment to be used:** Simple (transfer, payment order, check, etc.), as documentary (letter of credit, documentary collection, etc.)

Incoterms CPT obligations of the parties.

Salesman:

- Notify the buyer that the goods have been delivered to the carrier and that they have begun to move.

  - Deliver the goods to the main carrier, with the value of the international freight paid.
  - Pay all costs until the goods have been delivered to the main carrier, including those generated by customs clearance in the country of origin and the value of the international freight.
  - Generate evidence of conformity or proof of delivery of the goods, and when in charge, the seller shall deliver the transport documents with the date of departure, when the originals are printed, or provide assistance to the buyer to obtain the corresponding transport document or its proof.
  - Provide a commercial invoice and packing list, or an equivalent electronic document
  - To assist the buyer, ensuring the availability of services, information and complementary or additional documentation for the international traffic of goods.

  Buyer:

  - Provide sufficient information to the seller to perform the transfer or shipment of the cargo.
  - Receive the goods in conformity, after having been loaded on the means of transport.
  - Assume all costs and risks of the international traffic of the goods that are generated since they are loaded in the means of transport, except the value of the international freight.

- ☐ To receive the documents or receipts in conformity.

- ☐ Pay the price of the goods as agreed.

- ☐ Pay for additional services or documents requested from the seller.

Incoterms CPT costs and risks:

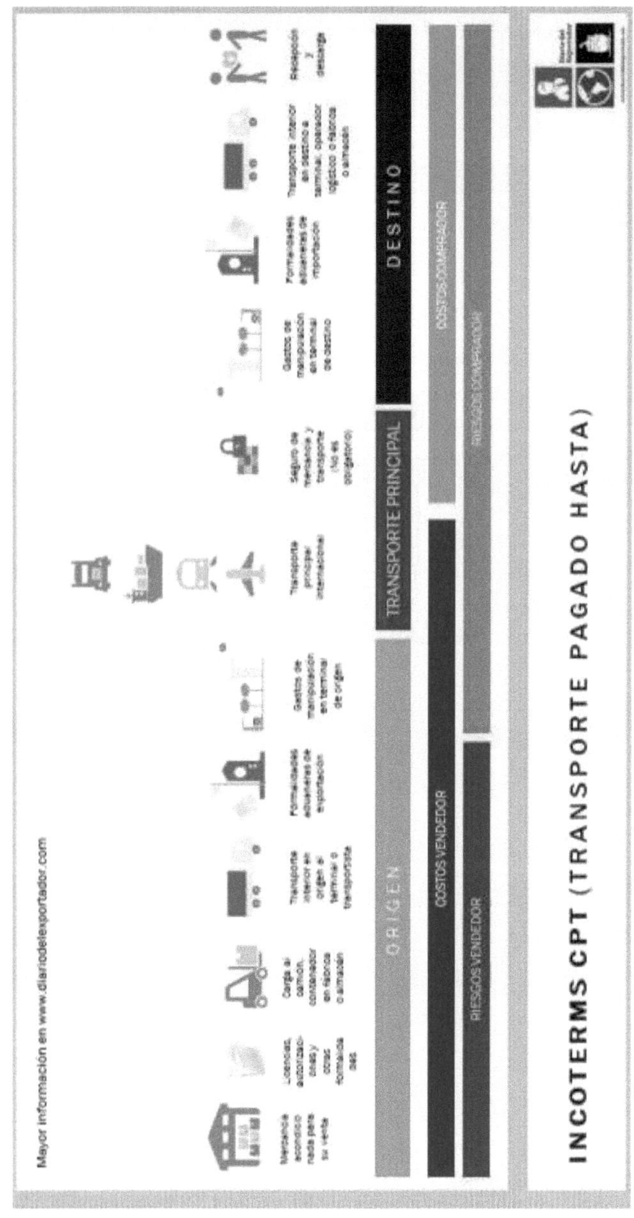

CPT Incoterms in the contract;

Since the transfer of risk and distribution of logistics and customs costs is dependent on the place of delivery, it is essential to specify the place of delivery of the goods as clearly as possible in the contract and pro forma invoice. The International Chamber of Commerce recommends the following structure: **The term Incoterms + place of delivery + Incoterms 2020 Rule**

Example: CPT, Mexico City International Airport, Aeromexico Cargo, Incoterms 2020

Notes and recommendations:

The term CPT allows for control over costs, goods, destination and deadlines, and a good margin for negotiation with customers. Even if the transport of the goods to the designated destination has to be paid, the risk is transferred at origin. As a disadvantage, there is no obligation for either party to insure the goods, which is not the case in CIP.

Incoterms CPT, as in the terms CIP, CFR or CIF, the transfer of risk and costs occur in different places. In other words, the exporter fulfils its delivery obligation when the goods are placed in the possession of the carrier (when several carriers are used to the agreed destination, the transfer occurs when the goods are delivered to the first of them) and not when the goods arrive at the place of destination. If the parties wish the risk to pass at a later stage (for example, at a port or airport), they need to specify this in the contract of sale.

The Incoterms type C terms are of interest to banks when letters of credit are involved, because they request that they be the consignee of the bill of lading. In this way they are the owners of the goods until the importer pays.

It is recommended that the agreed-upon destination of the goods be clearly established.

The term CIP stands for "Carriage and Insurance Paid To. In a sale and purchase transaction under the CIP term, the seller contracts and pays the costs of transportation needed to bring the goods to the designated place of destination, as well as the costs related to export clearance. In addition, the seller contracts **for comprehensive insurance** coverage **(Clause A)** against the buyer's risk of loss of or damage to the goods during carriage. The risks of loss and damage pass to the buyer from the moment the goods are delivered to the carrier's custody.

In the term CIP, risk is transmitted and costs are transferred in different places. It is therefore important that the seller and the buyer clearly specify both the place of delivery, where the risk is transferred to the buyer, and the designated place of destination to which the seller must contract for transport.

Incoterms CIP features:

- **Type of transport:** Any means of transport, including multimodal (containers)
- **Place of delivery:** At the point that the goods are delivered to the first carrier that the seller has contracted.
- **Location of the goods (loading/unloading):** Loaded on the first means of transport contracted by the seller.
- **Delivery document:** Transport document (CRM, CIM, B/L, AWB or DTM) and transport insurance policy
- **Type of cargo:** Any type of cargo (general, complete and groupage).

- **Hiring of the main transport:** Seller.

- **Contracting transport insurance:** The seller is obliged to contract transport insurance (Clause A of the *Institute Cargo Clauses*) in which the buyer is the beneficiary.
- **Transfer of risk from seller to buyer:** When the goods are delivered to the first carrier contracted by the seller.
- **Pre-shipment inspection:** Buyer, unless required by the seller's country in which case it will be at the seller's expense.
- **Export clearance:** Seller.

- **Import clearance:** Buyer.

- **Means of payment to be used:** Simple (transfer, payment order, check, etc.), as documentary (letter of credit, documentary collection, etc.)

Incoterms CIP obligations of the parties.

Salesman:

- Notify the buyer that the goods have been delivered to the carrier and that they have begun to move.
- Deliver the goods to the main carrier, with the value of the freight and international insurance paid.

- Pay all costs until the goods have been delivered to the principal carrier, including those arising from customs clearance in the country of origin, freight value and international insurance.
- The insurance to be taken out in favour of the exporter is 110% Clause A [all risk].

- Provide a commercial invoice and packing list, or an equivalent electronic document

- Generate evidence of conformity or proof of delivery of the goods, and when in charge, the seller must deliver the transport documents with the date of departure, when the originals are printed, and the insurance policy, or provide assistance to the buyer in obtaining the corresponding documents or proofs.
- To assist the buyer, ensuring the availability of services, information and complementary or additional documentation for the international traffic of goods.

Buyer:

- Provide sufficient information to the seller to perform the transfer or shipment of the cargo.
- Receive the goods in conformity, after having been loaded on the means of transport.
- Assume all costs and risks of international traffic of goods that are generated since they are loaded on the means of transport, except the values of freight and international insurance.
- Pay the price of the goods as agreed.
- To receive the documents or receipts in conformity.
- Pay for additional services or documents requested from the seller.

Incoterms CIP costs and risk:

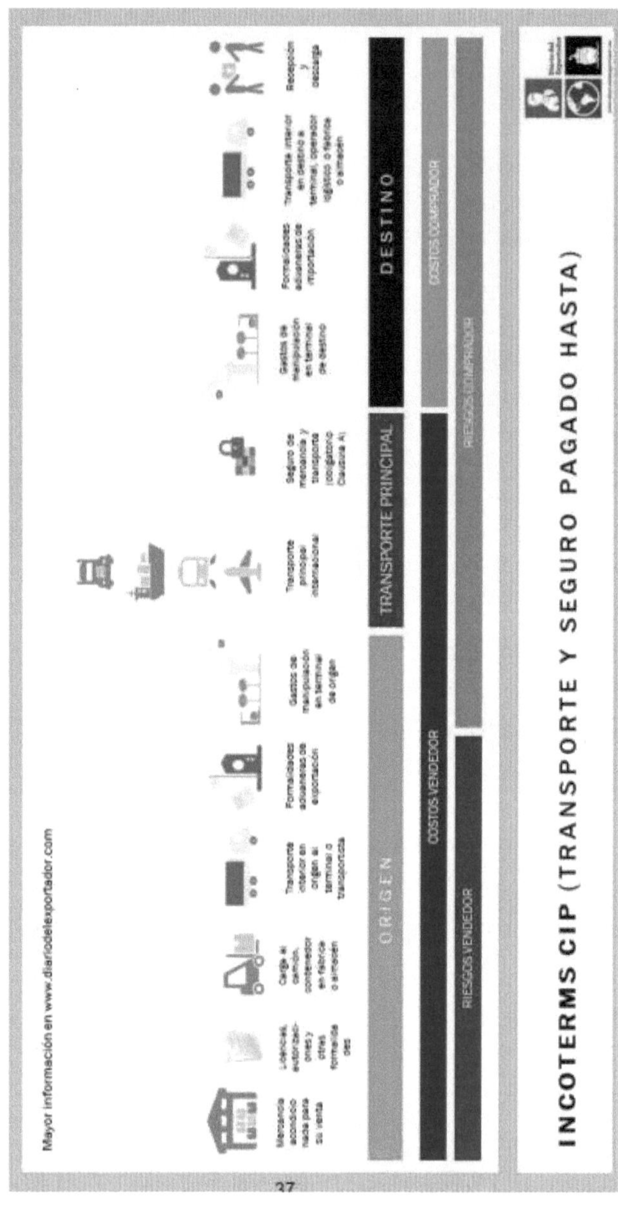

CIP Incoterms in the contract:

Since the transfer of risk and distribution of logistics and customs costs is dependent on the place of delivery, it is essential to specify the place of delivery of the goods as clearly as possible in the contract and pro forma invoice. The International Chamber of Commerce recommends the following structure: **The term Incoterms + place of delivery + Incoterms 2020 Rule**

Notes and recommendations:

Although transport is included in the sales price, the risks on the crossing are the buyer's.

It is recommended that the agreed-upon destination of the goods be clearly established.

The insurance is contracted by the seller, agreeing the conditions with the buyer. Although the insurance is contracted by the seller, the beneficiary must be the buyer who has the risk of the crossing. In the event of a claim, the insurance should be payable in the country of destination in the currency agreed upon in the transaction.

Coverage in the case of shipping is recommended to be 110% of the purchase value.

The Incoterms type C terms are of interest to banks when letters of credit are involved, because they request that they be the consignee of the bill of lading. In this way they are the owners of the goods until the importer pays.

The term CIF stands for "Cost Insurance and Freight". In a sales transaction under the CIF term, the seller delivers the goods on board the ship, and at that time the risk of loss or damage to the goods is transferred. The seller must contract and pay the costs and freight necessary to bring the goods to the named port of destination, and also contracts **for minimum insurance coverage (Clause C)** against the buyer's risk of loss of or damage to the goods during carriage, as well as the costs related to export clearance.

Characteristics Incoterms CIF:

- **Type of transport:** Exclusively for sea transport. Not recommended for multimodal transport (containers).
- **Place of delivery:** On board the vessel at the port of shipment designated by the seller.
- **Location of goods (loading/unloading):** On board **the** vessel designated by the seller.
- **Delivery document:** Bill of Lading (B/L) with mention of *freight prepaid,* and transport insurance policy.
- **Type of cargo:** Preferably general cargo operations
- **Hiring of the main transport:** Seller.
- **Taking out transport insurance:** The seller is obliged to take out transport insurance (Clause C of the Institute Cargo Clauses) in which the buyer is the beneficiary.
- **Transfer of risk from the seller to the buyer:** Once the goods have

been placed on board the ship, in the port designated by the seller.

- ☐ **Pre-shipment inspection:** Buyer, unless required by the seller's country in which case it will be at the seller's expense.
- ☐ **Export clearance:** Seller.
- ☐ **Import clearance:** Buyer.
- ☐ **Means of payment to be used:** Simple (transfer, payment order, check, etc.), as documentary (letter of credit, documentary collection, etc.)

☐

Incoterms CIF obligations of the parties.

Salesman:

- ☐ Notify the delivery of the goods on board the agreed vessel.
- ☐ Deliver the goods on board the agreed vessel with the value of the freight and international insurance paid.
    - ☐ Pay all costs until the cargo has been placed on the vessel that will move it to its destination, including those generated by customs clearance in the country of origin, the value of the freight and international insurance.
    - ☐ The insurance to be taken out in favour of the exporter is 110% Clause C [minimum risk]
    - ☐ Provide a commercial invoice and packing list, or an equivalent electronic document
    - ☐ Generate evidence of conformity or proof of delivery of the goods, and when in charge, the seller must deliver the transport documents with the date of shipment, when the originals are printed, and the insurance policy, or provide assistance to the buyer to obtain the corresponding documents or proofs.
    - ☐ To assist the buyer, ensuring the availability of services, information and complementary or additional documentation for the international traffic of goods.

Buyer:

- ☐ Provide sufficient information to the seller to perform the transfer or shipment of the cargo.
- ☐ Receive the goods in conformity, after they have been loaded on the

ship.

- [ ] Assume all costs and risks of the international traffic of goods generated since they are loaded on the ship, except the values of freight and international insurance.

- [ ] Pay the price of the goods as agreed.

- [ ] To receive the documents or receipts in conformity.

- [ ] Pay for additional services or documents requested from the seller.

Incoterms CIF costs and risks:

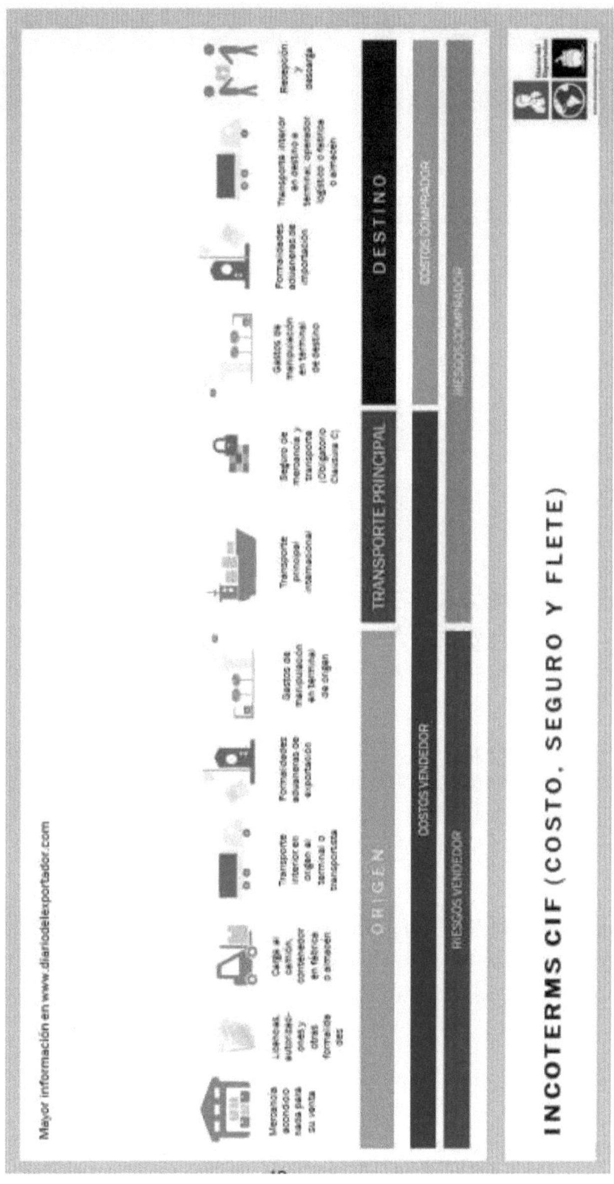

Incoterms CIF in the contract:

Since the transfer of risk and distribution of logistics and customs costs is dependent on the place of delivery, it is essential to specify the place of delivery of the goods as clearly as possible in the contract and pro forma invoice. The International Chamber of Commerce recommends the following structure: **The term Incoterms + place of delivery + Incoterms 2020 Rule**

Example: CIF, Port of Hamburg, Germany, Incoterms 2020

Notes and recommendations:

The use of CIF is totally recommendable because the costs are controllable and identifiable, the control of a great part of the operation is assumed having more margin of negotiation, the risk is transmitted in origin and a greater control is had on the merchandise, its destiny, the terms and the search of alternatives before unforeseen events.

In addition, it has the added bonus of being able to count on the certainty that you are transporting goods with contracted insurance. In this case, with minimum coverage ICC (C), lower than the coverage required in CIP which is ICC (A) and that we recommend as the best alternative to CIF), since in CPT and CFR there is no obligation for any of the parties to insure the goods. We insist that the use of CIF should only be used for sea transport, if land transport is also involved, the correct thing to do is to use the intermodal CIP.

The insurance is contracted by the seller, agreeing the conditions with the buyer. Although the insurance is contracted by the seller, the beneficiary must be the buyer who has the risk of the crossing. In the event of a claim, the insurance should be payable in the country of destination in the currency agreed upon in the transaction.

The Incoterms type C terms are of interest to banks when letters of credit are involved, because they request that they be the consignee of the bill of lading. In this way they are the owners of the goods until the importer pays.

The term CFR stands for "Cost and Freight". In a sale and purchase transaction under the CFR term, the seller delivers the goods on board the vessel. The risk of loss or damage to the goods is transferred when the goods are on board the ship. The seller must contract and pay the costs and freight necessary to bring the goods to the named port of destination, as well as the costs related to export clearance.

Incoterms CFR features:

- **Type of transport:** Exclusively for sea transport. Not recommended for multimodal transport (containers).
- **Place of delivery:** On board the vessel at the port of shipment designated by the seller.
- **Location of goods (loading/unloading):** On board **the** vessel designated by the seller.
  - **Delivery document:** Bill of Lading (B/L) with mention of *freight prepaid*.
  - **Type of cargo:** Preferably general cargo operations
  - **Hiring of the main transport:** Seller.
  - **Taking out transport insurance:** There is no obligation for either party. However, it is advisable for the buyer to take out insurance, since he is the one who assumes the risk in international transport.
  - **Transfer of risk from the seller to the buyer:** Once the goods have been placed on board the ship, in the port designated by the seller.
  - **Pre-shipment inspection:** Buyer, unless required by the seller's country

in which case it will be at the seller's expense.

- **Export clearance:** Seller.

- **Import clearance:** Buyer.

- **Means of payment to be used:** Simple (transfer, payment order, check, etc.), as documentary (letter of credit, documentary collection, etc.)

Incoterms CFR obligations of the parties.

Salesman:

- Notify the delivery of the goods on board the agreed vessel.

- Deliver the goods on board the agreed vessel.

- Pay all costs until the cargo has been placed on the vessel that will move it to its destination, including those generated by customs clearance in the country of origin and the value of the international freight.

- Generate evidence of conformity or proof of delivery of the goods, and when in charge, the seller must deliver the transport documents with the date of shipment, when the originals are printed, or provide assistance to the buyer to obtain the corresponding transport document or its proof.

- Provide a commercial invoice and packing list, or an equivalent electronic document

- To assist the buyer, ensuring the availability of services, information and complementary or additional documentation for the international traffic of goods.

Buyer:

- Provide sufficient information to the seller to perform the transfer or shipment of the cargo.

- Receive the goods in conformity, after they have been loaded on the ship.

- Assume all costs and risks of the international traffic of the goods generated since they are loaded on the ship, except the value of the international freight.

- To receive the documents or receipts in conformity.

- Pay the price of the goods as agreed.

- Pay for additional services or documents requested from the seller.

Incoterms CFR costs and risks:

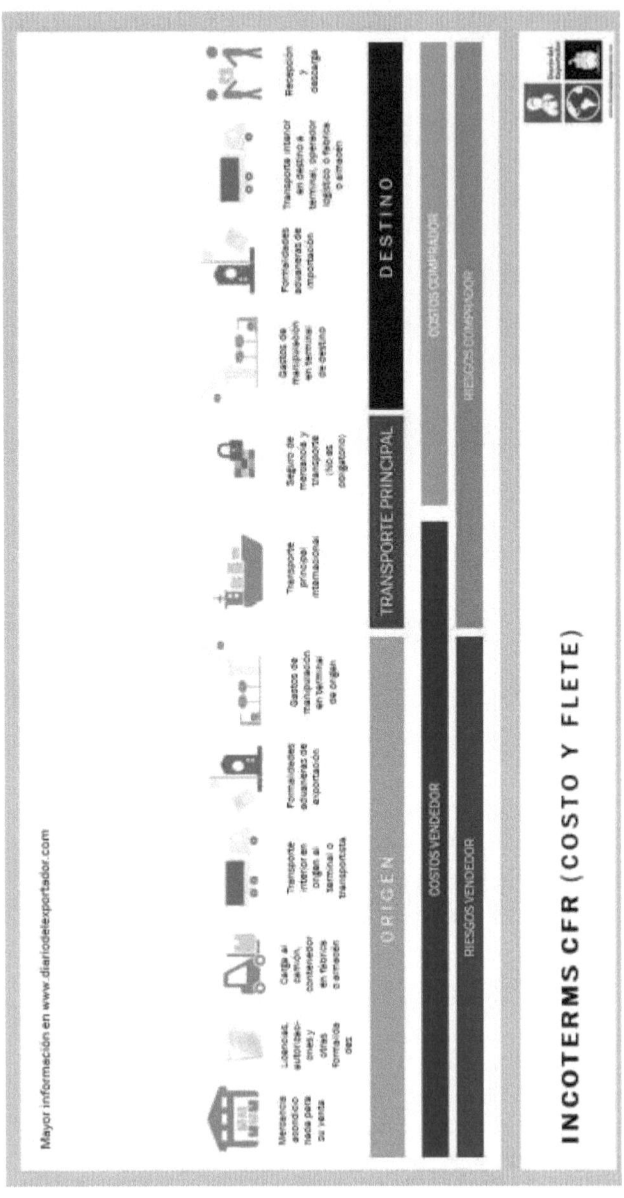

Incoterms CFR in the contract:

Since the transfer of risk and distribution of logistics and customs costs is dependent on the place of delivery, it is essential to specify the place of delivery of the goods as clearly as possible in the contract and pro forma invoice. The International Chamber of Commerce recommends the following structure: **The term Incoterms + place of delivery + Incoterms 2020 Rule**

Example: CFR, Rotterdam, Netherlands Incoterms 2020 rules

Notes and recommendations:

CFR, is highly recommended for the seller, because the costs are totally controllable and identifiable, it assumes control of much of the operation having more margin for negotiation, the risk is transmitted at the source and has greater control over the goods, their destination, deadlines and the search for alternatives to unforeseen events.

CFR may not be appropriate when the goods are placed in the possession of the carrier before they are on board the vessel, as is the case, for example, with containerised goods, which are usually delivered to a terminal. In such situations, the CPT rule should be used.

In the case of claiming international transport insurance coverage, the buyer must arrange it at his own expense.

The Incoterms type C terms are of interest to banks when letters of credit are involved, because they request that they be the consignee of the bill of lading. In this way they are the owners of the goods until the importer pays.

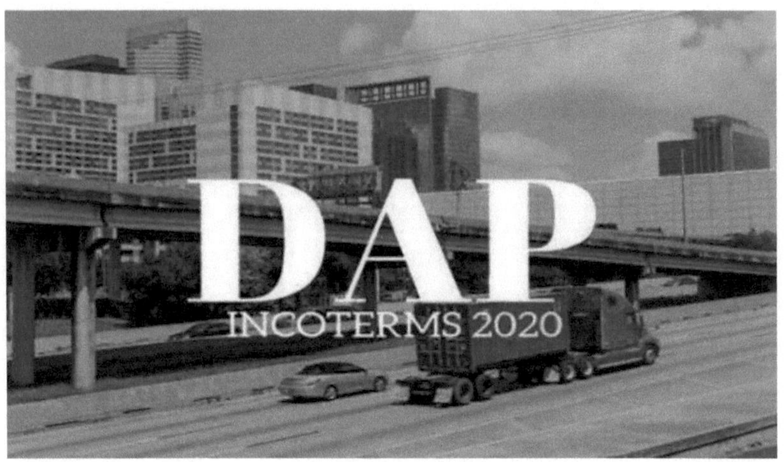

The term DAP stands for "Delivered *At* Place". In a sales transaction under the term DAP the seller delivers the goods on the arrival means of transport ready for unloading at the designated place of destination. The seller bears all risks involved in bringing the goods to the named place of destination, as well as the costs associated with the export clearance.

Incoterms DAP features:

- **Type of transport:** Any means of transport, including multimodal (containers)
- **Place of delivery:** At the buyer's own premises (factory or warehouse) in the country of destination; or At an inland point in the country of destination.
- **Location of the goods (loading/unloading):** Ready for unloading at the delivery place designated by the buyer.
- **Delivery document:** Delivery document signed by the buyer; or Delivery document signed by the buyer's carrier.
- **Type of cargo:** Any type of cargo (general, complete and groupage).
- **Hiring of the main transport:** Seller.
- **Taking out transport insurance:** There is no obligation for either party. However, it is advisable that the seller contracts it since it is the one who assumes the risk in international transport.
- **Transfer of risk from seller to buyer:** When the goods are delivered

ready for unloading from the means of transport at the designated place at destination.

- **Pre-shipment inspection:** Buyer, unless required by the seller's country in which case it will be at the seller's expense.
- **Export clearance:** Seller.
- **Import clearance:** Buyer.
- **Means of payment to be used:** Simple (transfer, payment order, check, etc.)

Incoterms DAP obligations of the parties.

Salesman:

- Notify the buyer that the goods have arrived at the agreed-upon location at the destination.
  - Placing the goods at the disposal of the buyer at the agreed location, within the time and terms established, the seller is not obliged to unload the goods at the agreed place.
  - Pay all costs until the goods are placed at the disposal of the buyer in the agreed location, except the costs for customs clearance in the country of destination.
  - Generate evidence of conformity or proof of delivery of the goods, and when in charge, provide the buyer with all documents generated in international transit necessary to initiate customs clearance at destination, or provide assistance in obtaining them.
  - Provide a commercial invoice and packing list, or an equivalent electronic document
  - To assist the buyer, ensuring the availability of services, information and complementary or additional documentation for the international traffic of goods.

Buyer:

  - Provide sufficient information to the seller to perform the transfer or shipment of the cargo.
  - Receive the goods in conformity, once they have arrived at the agreed location.
  - Assume all costs and risks of the international traffic of the goods that are generated since they arrive at the agreed location at the destination, including the unloading of the goods.
  - Receive the documents in conformity.

☐ Pay the price of the goods as agreed.

☐ Pay for additional services or documents requested from the seller.

48

Incoterms DAP costs and risks:

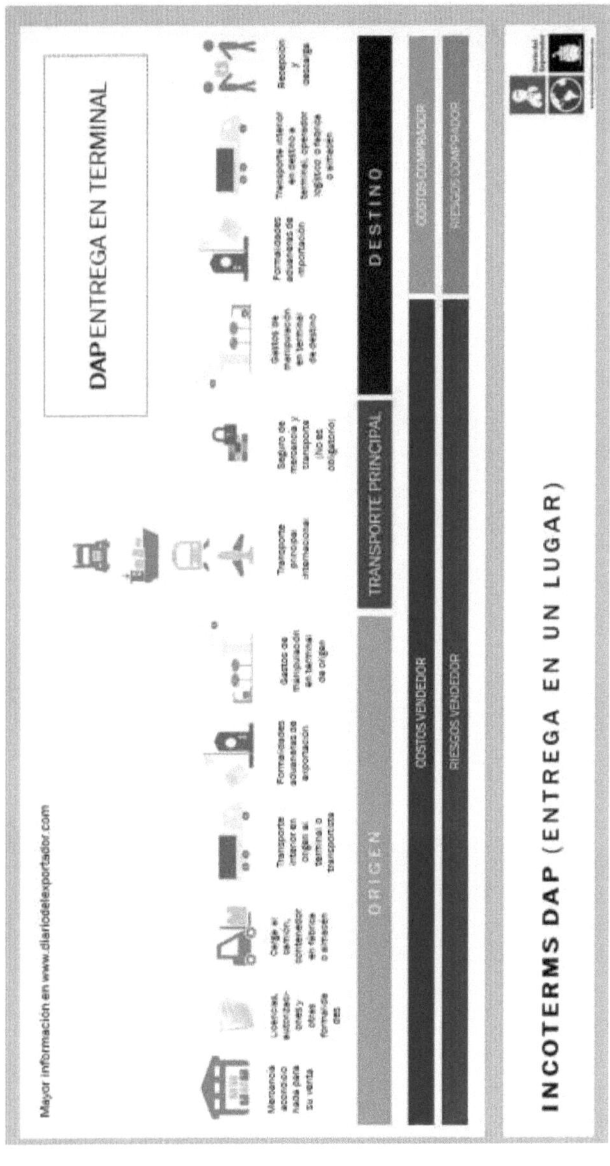

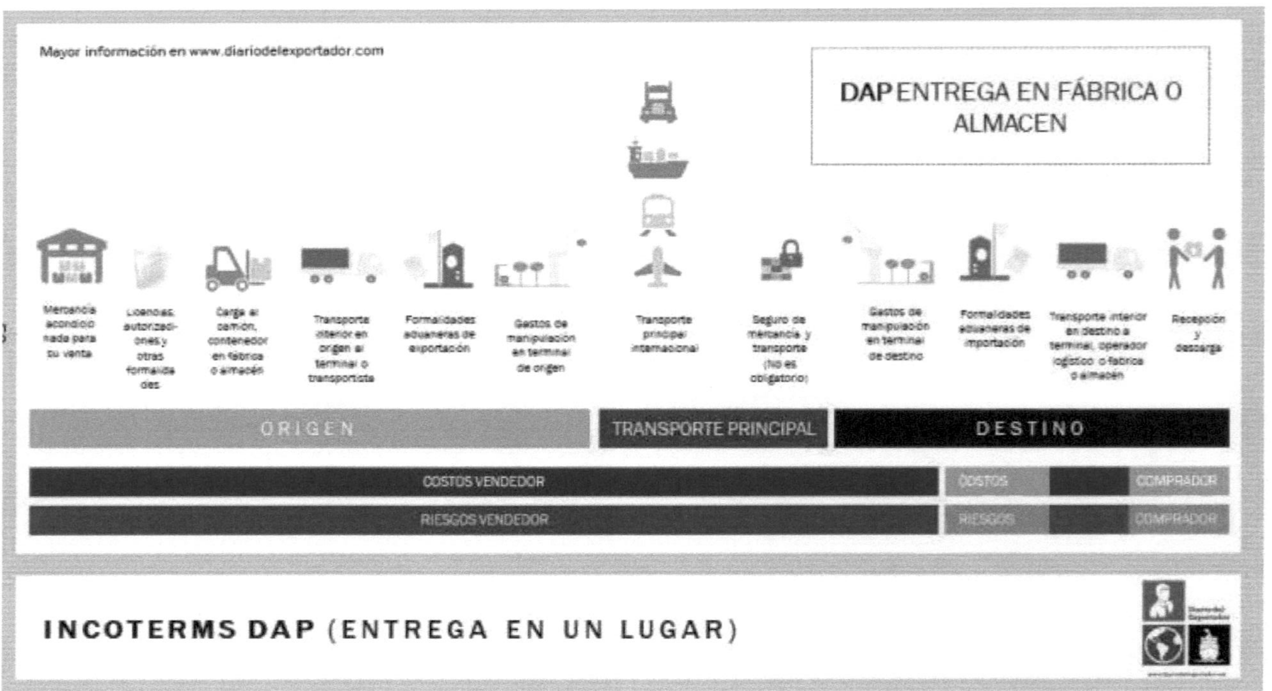

Mayor información en www.diariodelexportador.com
DAP ENTREGA EN FÁBRICA O ALMACEN
Mercancía acondicionada para su venta
Licencias, autorizaciones y otras formalidades
Carga al camión, contenedor en fábrica o almacén
Transporte interior en origen al terminal o transportista
Formalidades aduaneras de exportación
Gastos de manipulación en terminal de origen
Transporte principal internacional
Seguro de mercancía y transporte (no es obligatorio)
Gastos de manipulación en terminal de destino
Formalidades aduaneras de importación
Transporte interior en destino a terminal, operador logístico o fábrica o almacén
Recepción y descarga
ORIGEN
TRANSPORTE PRINCIPAL
DESTINO
COSTOS VENDEDOR
COSTOS
COMPRADOR
RIESGOS VENDEDOR
RIESGOS
COMPRADOR
INCOTERMS DAP (ENTREGA EN UN LUGAR)

Incoterms DAP in the contract:

Since the transfer of risk and distribution of logistics and customs costs is dependent on the place of delivery, it is essential to specify the place of delivery of the goods as clearly as possible in the contract and pro forma invoice. The International Chamber of Commerce recommends the following structure: **The term Incoterms + place of delivery + Incoterms 2020 Rule**

Example: DAP, Hong Kong by Air, Incoterms 2020

Notes and recommendations:

In view of the responsibility and the route to be covered by the seller, we do not recommend this term Incoterms in developing countries that do not have an optimal infrastructure, where there is a real possibility of suffering any setback, causing the costs to be very difficult to control. In these cases we recommend more the use of CIP (if it is a multimodal transport) or CIF (if it is only maritime transport) where the risk is transmitted in origin and the contracting of a goods insurance is obligatory.

The term DPU stands for "Delivered at Place Unloaded". In a sales transaction under the term DPU, the seller delivers the goods when he makes them available to the buyer on the arrival means of transport, unloaded by his own means, and at the agreed-upon point of destination.

The seller bears all risks involved in bringing the goods to the designated point of destination and unloading them there, as well as the costs related to export clearance.

It is the only Incoterms term that obliges the seller to unload at destination.

Incoterms DPU features.

Type of transport: Any means of transport, including multimodal (containers)

Place of delivery: At the buyer's own premises (factory or warehouse) in the country of destination; or At an inland point in the country of destination.

Location of the goods (loading/unloading): Unloaded from the means of transport that the seller has contracted to take the goods to the place of delivery designated by the buyer.

Delivery document: Delivery document signed by the buyer; or Delivery document signed by the buyer's carrier.

Type of cargo: Any type of cargo (general, complete and groupage).

Hiring of the main transport: Seller.

Taking out transport insurance: There is no obligation for either party. However, it is advisable that the seller contracts it since it is the one who assumes the risk in international transport.

Transfer of risk from seller to buyer: When the goods have been unloaded from the transport market contracted by the seller at the designated place at destination.

Pre-shipment inspection: Buyer, unless required by the seller's country in which case it will be at the seller's expense.

Export clearance: Seller.

Import clearance: Buyer.

Means of payment to be used: Simple (transfer, payment order, check, etc.)

Incoterms DPU obligations of the parties. Seller:

- Notify the buyer that the goods have been unloaded at the agreed-upon location at the destination.
- Place the goods at the disposal of the buyer, unloaded at the agreed location, in the established times and terms.
- Pay all costs until the goods are unloaded at the agreed upon location, except for the costs of customs clearance in the country of destination.
- Generate evidence of conformity or proof of delivery of the goods, and when in charge, provide the buyer with all documents generated in international transit necessary to initiate customs clearance at destination, or provide assistance in obtaining them.
- Provide a commercial invoice and packing list, or an equivalent electronic document
- To assist the buyer, ensuring the availability of services, information and complementary or additional documentation for the international traffic of goods.

Buyer:

- Provide sufficient information to the seller to perform the transfer or shipment of the cargo.
- Receive the goods in conformity, once they have been unloaded in the

agreed location.

- ☐ Assume all costs and risks of the international traffic of the goods that are generated since they are unloaded in the agreed location at the destination.

- ☐ Receive the documents in conformity.

- ☐ Pay the price of the goods as agreed.

- ☐ Pay for additional services or documents requested from the seller.

Incoterms DPU costs and risks:

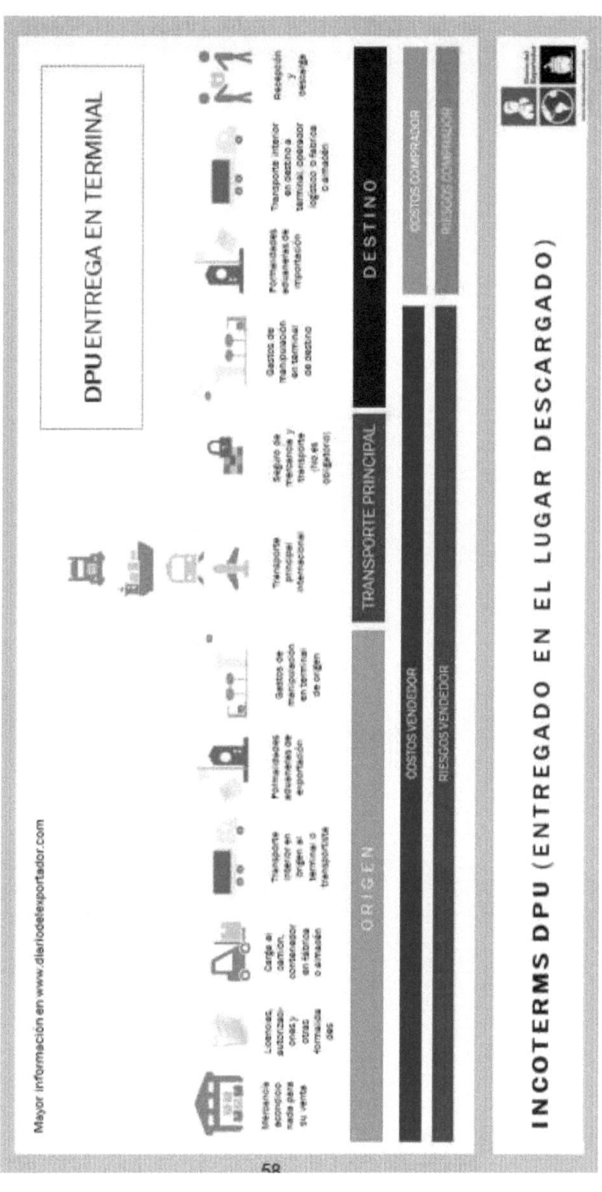

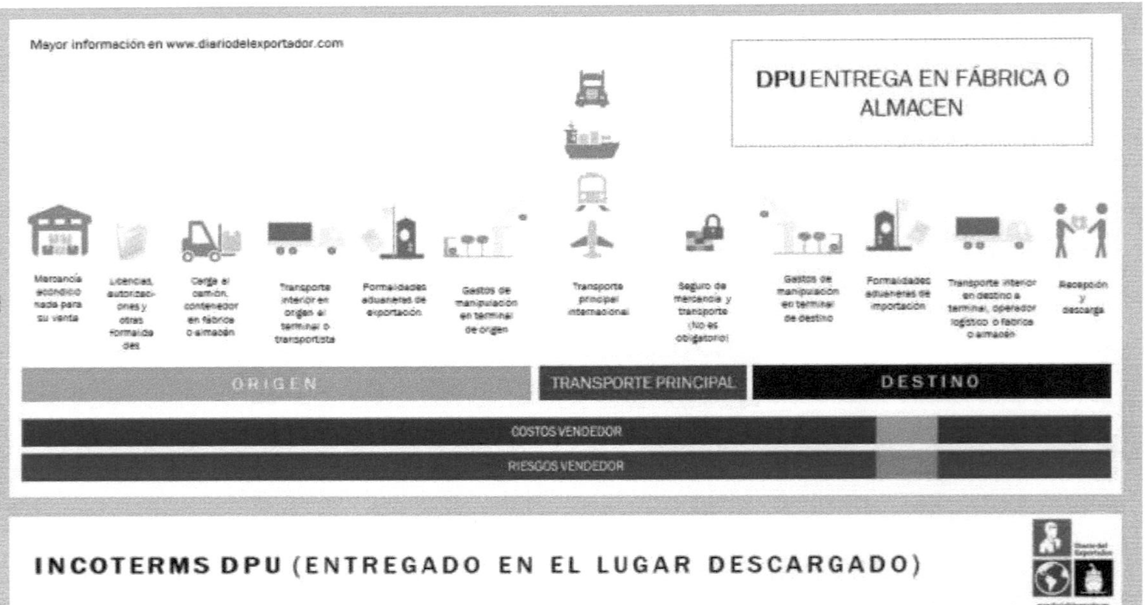

Mayor información en www.diariodelexportador.com
DPU ENTREGA EN FÁBRICA O ALMACEN
Mercancía acondicionada para su venta
Licencias, autorizaciones y otras formalidades
Carga el camión, contenedor en fábrica o almacén
Transporte interior en origen al terminal o transportista
Formalidades aduaneras de exportación
Gastos de manipulación en terminal de origen
Transporte principal internacional
Seguro de mercancía y transporte (no es obligatorio)
Gastos de manipulación en terminal de destino
Formalidades aduaneras de importación
Transporte interior en destino a terminal, operador logístico o fábrica o almacén
Recepción y descarga
ORIGEN
TRANSPORTE PRINCIPAL
DESTINO
COSTOS VENDEDOR
RIESGOS VENDEDOR
INCOTERMS DPU (ENTREGADO EN EL LUGAR DESCARGADO)

Incoterms DPU in the contract:

Since the transfer of risk and distribution of logistics and customs costs is dependent on the place of delivery, it is essential to specify the place of delivery of the goods as clearly as possible in the contract and pro forma invoice. The International Chamber of Commerce recommends the following structure: **The term Incoterms + place of delivery + Incoterms 2020 Rule**

Example: DPU, Block C, TingDao Plaza, Dunhua Road No. 380, Qingdao City, Shandong Province China, Incoterms 2020

Notes and recommendations:

Incoterms DPU is designed for companies that want to control the logistic chain from origin to destination due to the particularities of their business or merchandise, or where they have to carry out the implementation of the sold merchandise in the buyer's facilities.

As with DAP, in view of the responsibility and the route to be covered by the seller, we do not recommend this term in countries with underdeveloped transport and telecommunications infrastructures, where there is a real possibility of suffering any setback, causing the costs to be very difficult to control.

In these cases, we recommend more the use of CIP (if it is a multimodal transport) or CIF (if it is only maritime transport) where the risk is transmitted at origin and it is mandatory to contract a goods insurance (taking into account the different coverage that applies from the version of INCOTERMS 2020).

Likewise, we do not recommend the use of this Incoterms even in much more developed countries if we do not have the 100% security of having sufficient means and personnel to carry out the unloading of the goods at destination, due to the extra costs and risk of damage to the goods that can be caused.

The term DDP stands for "Delivered Duty Paid. In a sales transaction under the DDP term the seller delivers the goods, cleared for import on the arrival means of transport, ready for unloading at the named place of destination. The seller bears all risks involved in bringing the goods to the terminal at the named port or place of destination and unloading them there, as well as the costs associated with export and import clearance.

Incoterms DDP features:

Type of transport: Any means of transport, including multimodal (containers)

Place of delivery: At the buyer's own premises (factory or warehouse) in the country of destination; or At an inland point in the country of destination.

Location of the goods (loading/unloading): Ready for unloading at the delivery place designated by the buyer.

Delivery document: Delivery document signed by the buyer; or Delivery document signed by the buyer's carrier.

Type of cargo: Any type of cargo (general, complete and groupage).

Hiring of the main transport: Seller.

Taking out transport insurance: There is no obligation for either party. However, it is advisable that the seller contracts it since it is the one who assumes the risk in international transport.

Transfer of risk from seller to buyer: When the goods are delivered ready for unloading from the means of transport at the designated place at destination.

Pre-shipment   inspection:
Seller. **Export   clearance:**
Seller. **Import   clearance:**
Seller.
Means of payment to be used: Simple (transfer, payment order, check, etc.)

Incoterms DDP obligations of the parties.

Salesman:

- Notify the buyer that the goods have cleared customs and arrived at the agreed-upon location at the destination.
    - To deliver the goods to the buyer, with the customs clearance process completed, at the agreed location at the place of destination, in the time and terms established, it is not the buyer's obligation to unload the goods at the agreed location.
    - Pay all costs until the goods are delivered to the buyer, including costs for customs clearance in the country of destination.
    - Deliver the original documentation of the goods.
    - Manage the export of the cargo at origin and manage the import of the goods at destination

Buyer:

- Provide sufficient information to the seller to perform the transfer or shipment of the cargo.
- Receive the goods in conformity, once they have been admitted to the place of destination and are available at the agreed location.
- Check the goods and receive them in conformity.
- To receive the documents or receipts in conformity.
- Provide additional or complementary local documentation for the admission of the goods to the place of destination. (where necessary)

Incoterms DDP costs and risks:

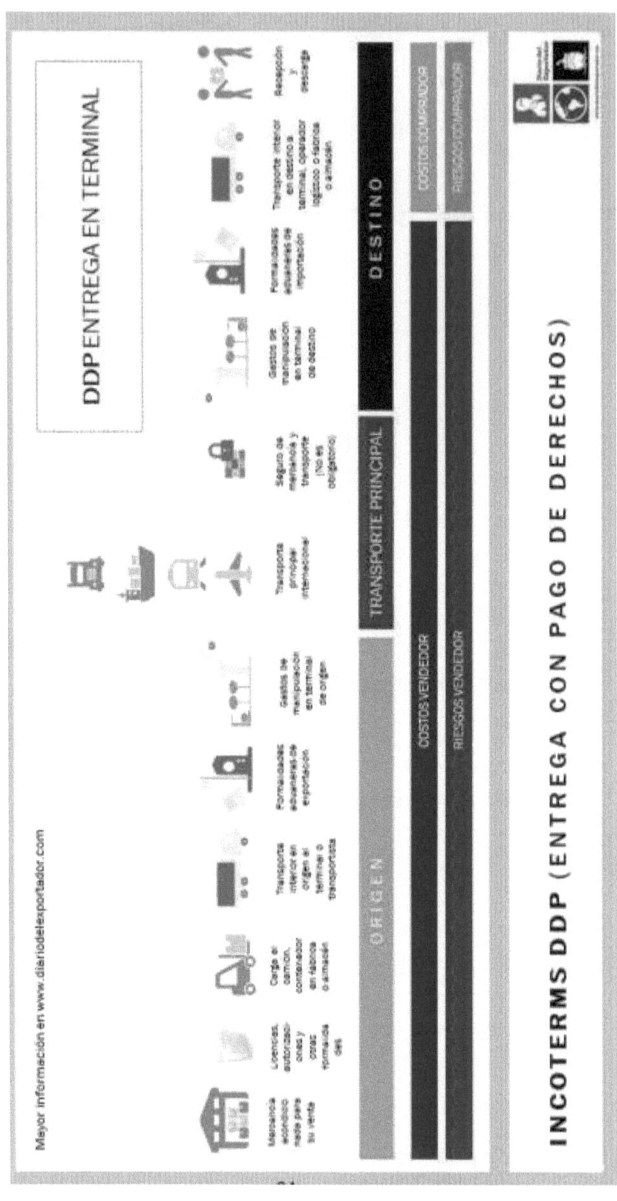

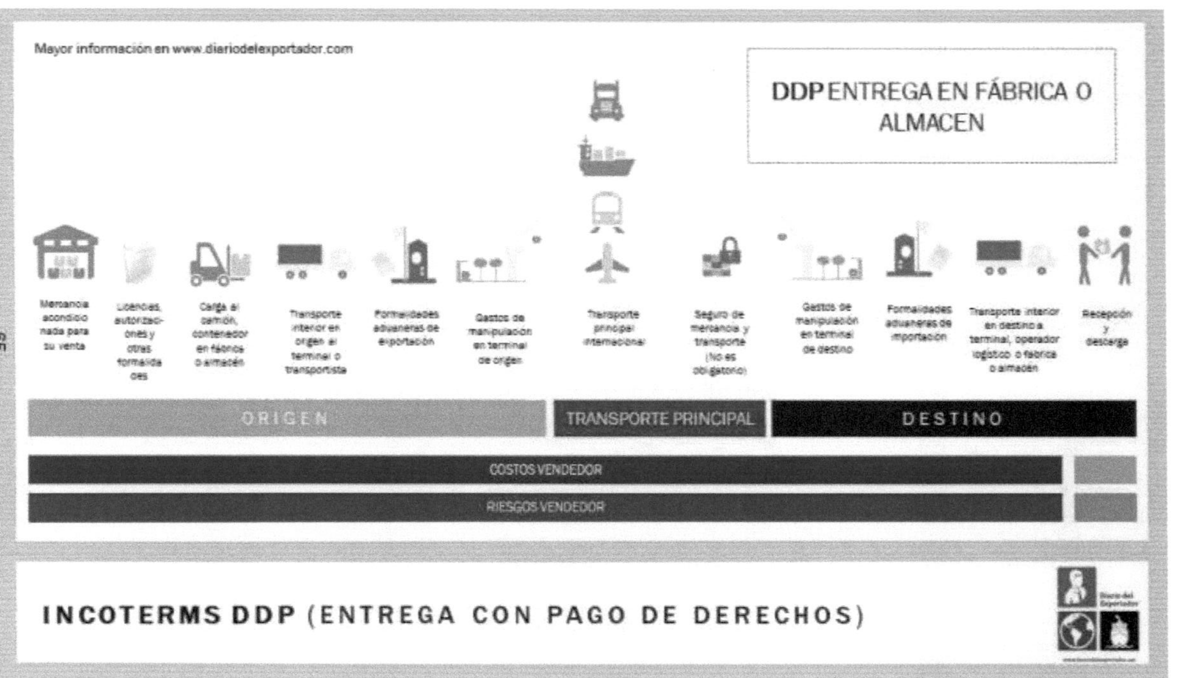

INCOTERMS DDP (ENTREGA CON PAGO DE DERECHOS)

DDP Incoterms in the contract:

Since the transfer of risk and distribution of logistics and customs costs is dependent on the place of delivery, it is essential to specify the place of delivery of the goods as clearly as possible in the contract and pro forma invoice. The International Chamber of Commerce recommends the following structure: ***The term Incoterms + place of delivery + Incoterms 2020 Rule***

Example: DDP, Frankfurt, Germany, Schmidt GmbH Warehouse 4, Incoterms 2020

Notes and recommendations:

DDP entails the greatest risk and responsibility for the seller, since not only does it oblige him to assume the cost of transport and risk from origin to the buyer's warehouse at destination, but he must also manage and pay the corresponding customs formalities and taxes in the country of destination. The only thing that does not oblige him is to unload the goods at the destination warehouse.

In addition, if the seller's company is not established in the country of destination, the taxes that may be deductible, as is the case with VAT in Ecuador, become costs that increase the price of the goods without any need.

Due to the above points, in addition to what we commented on with the Incoterms DAP, we recommend that exporters avoid this Incoterms when selling to third countries as long as the destination of the goods is not a country that allows 100% control of transport costs.

In general we recommend more the use of CIP (if it is a multimodal transport) or CIF (if it is only maritime transport) where the risk is transmitted at origin. In the case of opting for DDP, since we assume the risk until destination, it will be convenient for the seller to contract goods insurance, although he is not obliged to do so.

Summary:

El vendedor pone la mercancía a disposición del comprador:
IMPORTACIÓN
En punto convenido (descargar)
En punto convenido (sin descargar)
Grupo D
Llegada
DPU
DAP
DDP
* seguro de transporte
Grupo C
Transporte pagado
CPT
CIP
CFR
CIF
FOB
FAS
Grupo F
Transporte principal debido
FCA
EXPORTACIÓN
Grupo E
Salida
EXW
En locales del vendedor (sin cargar)
Al transportista convenido
Al costado del buque
A bordo del buque
INCOTERMS 2020 – DISTRIBUCIÓN DE COSTOS Y RIESGOS
Mayor información en www.diariodelexportador.com

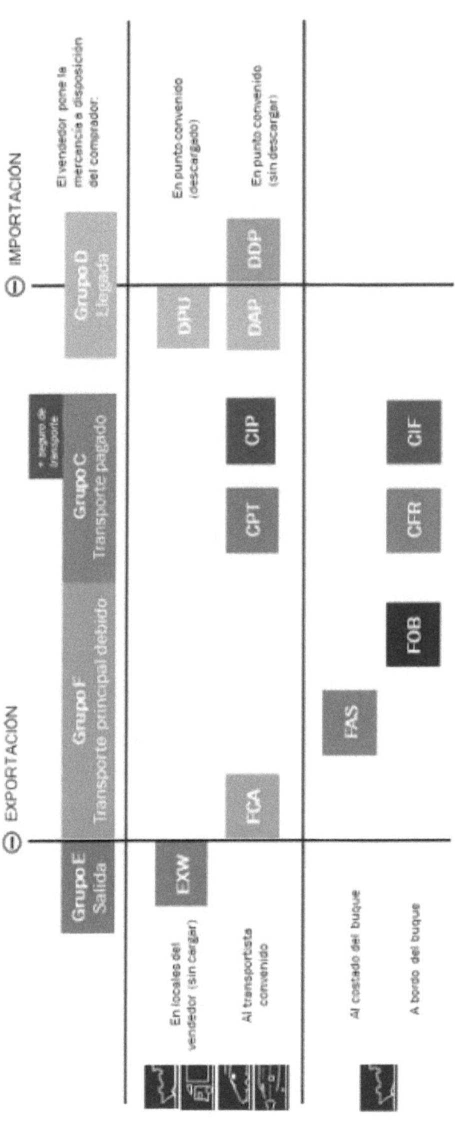

The Incoterms 2020 rules are a set of three-letter terms governing the responsibilities of companies in contracts for the sale of goods, accepted by governments, business people and professionals worldwide for the interpretation of the most common terms used in International Trade. Incoterms rules regulate the following:

- When and where the transfer of risk over.

- the goods, from the seller to the buyer.

- The place of delivery of the goods.

- Who hires and pays the transportation and insurance costs

- What documentation each party has to deal with.

It should be noted that the INCOTERMS rules do not last forever, but are regularly updated by the International Chamber of Commerce. In this last 2020 update, we can say that the modifications are minimal since there is a change of name from DAT (Delivered At Terminal) to DPU (Delivered at Place Unloaded), apparently because of the little use that companies have made of it and the restrictive vision that the concept "Terminal" supposed, despite the fact that it was indicated in the 2010 version that it was not only referred to maritime terminals. DPU is designed for those companies that are in charge of selling by project or very sensitive goods that require control of the entire logistics chain from loading at origin to unloading and operation at destination (with the exception of customs formalities and payment of taxes at destination).

However, in addition to the change of DAT to DPU, there have been minor changes to CIP/CIF and FCA. In CIP/CIF there are modifications in the insurance coverage: until now it was mandatory to take out a policy with at least ICC "C" coverage in both cases. With the implementation of the INCOTERMS 2020, if we agree to ship under CIP conditions the coverage must be ICC "A" (the so-called "all risks at sea") while if the shipment is made under CIF conditions the obligation to take out at least ICC "C" coverage (below class "A") remains.

As far as the FCA is concerned, the 2020 version provides the option, in case of maritime transport, for the buyer to instruct the carrier (shipping line or its agent) he has contracted to issue a Bill of Lading (B/L) in the name of the seller with the notation "on board", which indicates that the goods have been loaded on board the ship. This is the most common transport document used in the operation of letters of credit to justify the delivery of the goods and thus make payment to the seller.

The rest of the changes are of lesser significance, more "formal" and are related to the presentation of the information, the relation of costs, the obligation of the seller or buyer, when indicated by the term INCOTERMS to contract the transport (which was indicated until now) or to provide it by their own means (the novelty in INCOTERMS 2020 if they have their own fleet that does not require contracting third parties), the inclusion of requirements deriving from transport safety in a generic way (e.g. VGM) or the inclusion of explanatory notes which, until now, did not exist.

In the current 2020 version, the Incoterms rules are 11 terms and are divided into Incoterms for any mode of transport or multipurpose (EXW, FAC, CPT, CIP, DAP, DPU and DDP) and for maritime and inland waterway transport (FAS, FOB, CFR and CIF), each of which is explained briefly below:

Incoterms EXW:

The obligations of the seller/exporter end when the goods are placed at the disposal of the buyer/importer at his premises, at which time all costs are passed on to the buyer, the former being exempt from all liability, both for loading the goods and for customs export formalities. Mode of transport: Multipurpose.

The term EXW implies minimum obligations, however, by not controlling the customs clearance, we may have difficulties in obtaining the documents that justify the export. These documents (SAD) are necessary to justify the operation and not have problems with tax authorities (VAT or IGV).

Therefore, I recommend using EXW in operations between countries of the same economic or customs union (European Union) or between states or regions of a country where there are no customs procedures; or where the transport is Courier type (the package is normally loaded by the same carrier in his vehicle because it is usually small).

Incoterms FCA:

FCA is a very versatile term. We can use FCA Factory or FCA Terminal (port, airport, etc.).

FCA Factory (seller's premises): must be used for full loads (trailer or container). The seller must load the goods into the transport and from that moment on the goods become the responsibility of the buyer. The term FCA Factory perfectly replaces the term EXW, since it solves the risks and problems that it causes to the seller.

FCA Terminal (another place designated by the buyer): should be used only for split loads. The seller must deliver the goods only at the designated place. The unloading of the goods and their subsequent handling and consolidation in another transport are at the expense and risk of the buyer.

Use this term if the buyer gets better freight prices or if our knowledge of international trade is low.

When documentary payment mechanisms are included in the commercial transaction, the buyer can request the carrier to issue the B/L marked "on board" so that the seller can present it to the bank.

Incoterms FAS:

Delivery occurs in the country of origin, when the seller leaves the goods at the quay of the port and with the export clearance already done. At this place the seller's responsibility for damage or loss of the goods ends and the buyer is therefore liable. This does not include taking the goods on board the ship.

FOB Incoterms:

Delivery occurs in the country of origin, when the seller leaves the goods in the hold of the ship, loaded and stowed, and with the export clearance already done.

The responsibility of the seller for any damage or loss of the goods is transferred to the buyer once the goods have been declared on board the ship, which implies that the carrier has custody and control of the goods.

Incoterms CFR:

The main transport is paid by the seller, but the risk on this journey is the buyer's. The buyer must be aware that the insurance of the goods is at his expense. Delivery occurs when the goods are placed on board the ship, as in FOB, with the substantial difference that with CFR the seller must contract for international transport and pay the freight.

Incoterms CIF

The main transport is paid by the seller, but the irrigation in that stretch is the buyer's. The insurance of the goods is paid by the seller, who has to put the buyer as the beneficiary. Delivery occurs when the goods are placed on board the ship.

The seller is obliged to obtain insurance with minimum coverage in favour of the buyer (ICC C). However, other coverage can be arranged by prior agreement with the buyer. It is also common practice to cover 110% of the total cost of the transaction.

CPT Incoterms:

The main transport is paid by the seller, but the risk on this journey is the buyer's. If there are several carriers, it is when it is delivered to the 1st carrier at the point chosen by the seller, over which the buyer has no control. Specify in the contract if you want the risk to be transferred at a later stage.

CIP Incoterms:

The main transport and insurance is paid by the seller, but the risk on this journey is the buyer's. It is important for the buyer to be clear that the insurance of the goods is the responsibility of the seller, but that the seller assumes the risk from the moment the goods leave the country of origin, when they are delivered to the main carrier. The seller must put the buyer as the beneficiary of the insurance.

The seller is obliged to obtain insurance with maximum coverage in favour of the buyer (ICC A). However, other coverage can be arranged by prior agreement with the buyer. It is also common practice to cover 110% of the total cost of the transaction.

And just like the CPT term in the case of several carriers, it occurs when it is delivered to the 1st carrier at the point chosen by the seller, over which, the buyer has no control. Specify in the contract whether you want the risk to be transferred at a later stage.

DAP Incoterms:

Delivery is made anywhere in the country of destination, but always by vehicle (DAP factory, DAP carrier, etc.) and without import customs clearance.

In view of the responsibility and the route to be covered by the seller, we do not recommend this INCOTERM in developing countries, where there is a real possibility of suffering any setback, causing the expenses to be very difficult to control.

Incoterms DPU:

The delivery of the goods occurs in the country of destination without import clearance, at the agreed point of destination. This is the only Incoterms rule that obliges the seller to unload at destination.

This Incoterms is designed for companies that want to control the logistic chain from origin to destination due to the particularities of their business or merchandise, or where they have to carry out the implementation of the sold merchandise in the buyer's facilities.

As with DAP, in view of the responsibility and the route to be covered by the seller, we do not recommend this Incoterms in countries with underdeveloped transport and telecommunications infrastructures, where there is a real possibility of suffering any setback, causing expenses to be very difficult to control.

Incoterms DDP:

Delivery is made anywhere in the country of destination, but always by vehicle (DDP factory, DDP carrier, etc.). Within the price DDP are included the tariffs and internal taxes.

It is advisable to use DDP for low value goods where the transport used is Courier type. The aim is to provide a fast service to the customer who has an emergency, such as sending a part for a machine that the buyer has stopped. The aim is for the part to arrive quickly so that the factory can continue to operate. Here the important thing is not the cost but the urgency of the shipment.

COSTOS	EXW	FCA	CPT	CIP	DAP	DPU	DDP	FAS	FOB	CFR	CIF
- Embalaje y verificación	V	V	V	V	V	V	V	V	V	V	V
- Carga transporte interior	C	V/C	V	V	V	V	V	V	V	V	V
- Transporte interior origen	C	C	V	V	V	V	V	V	V	V	V
- Trámites de exportación	C	V	V	V	V	V	V	V	V	V	V
- THC en terminal origen	C	C	V	V	V	V	V	C	V	V	V
- Flete marítimo	C	C	V	V	V	V	V	C	C	V	V
- Seguro de transporte	(C)	(C)	(C)	V	(V)	(V)	(V)	(C)	(C)	(C)	V
- THC en terminal destino	C	C	C	C	V	V	V	C	C	C	C
- Trámites de importación	C	C	C	C	C	C	V	C	C	C	C
- Transporte interior destino	C	C	V/C	V/C	V	V	V	C	C	C	C
- Descarga lugar de destino	C	C	C	C	C	V	C	C	C	C	C

( ) Contrato de seguro de transporte opcional

INCOTERMS 2020 – DISTRIBUCIÓN DE COSTOS Y RIESGOS

Mayor información en www.dianodelexportador.com

Recommendations on the use of Incoterms® 2020 rules

Incoterms are a collection of internationally recognized standardized trade terms published by the International Chamber of Commerce (ICC) and widely used in national and international sales.

In September 2019, ICC published the latest version: Incoterms 2020, and the new rules entered into force on 1 January 2020. The changes made in Incoterms 2020 since the 2010 edition are largely presentational and explanatory. Substantive changes include:

A change in the term FCA (Free Carrier) Popular in the container trade, whereby the seller legally delivers the goods to the buyer before they are loaded onto a vessel and therefore cannot receive a bill of lading from the carrier, which requires payment under a letter of credit. The Incoterms FCA 2020 now contains an option under which the buyer agrees to instruct the carrier to issue the bill of lading to the seller.

Under the CIP (Carriage and Insurance Paid) term, the seller must now obtain a higher level of cargo insurance. Under Incoterms 2010, a CIP seller was required to purchase cargo insurance under the terms of the Institute's Cargo Clauses (C), which provides coverage for a limited number of risks. Under Incoterms 2020, a CIP seller must purchase insurance on the Institute's Cargo Clauses (A), which is an "all risks" policy with some exclusions.

The term 'DAT' has been changed to 'DPU', reflecting the fact that the destination for a delivery could be anywhere and not just a terminal. Of course, the place of delivery, if not a terminal, must be suitable for unloading the goods.

It is convenient that buyers and sellers take into account these changes in Incoterms 2020, it is also recommended to take into account the following points when adopting Incoterms 2020 in their operations.

Use of Incoterms in documents:

It is important to know that Incoterms® is not a generic name for any international trade term, but is a trademark used to mark the Rules designed by the International Chamber of Commerce (ICC). Therefore, it is extremely important to use Incoterms® in the right way: which means that you should always use the following exact notation
 - The name of the Incoterms® rule chosen,

 - The designated port, the place of destination or the agreed point

☐ Incoterms

☐ Year of issue

A correct notation therefore is:

☐ FCA 33 Avenue President Wilson, Paris, France, Incoterms® 2020

☐ DAP N0 123, ABC Street, Portland, Incoterms® 2020

☐ FOB Rotterdam, Incoterms® 2020

☐ CIF Shanghai, Incoterms® 2020

Accuracy in place of delivery or destination:

Try to be as precise as possible by indicating the place of delivery at origin or at destination, depending on the Incoterms chosen. In this way the responsibilities and obligations of the buyer and seller will be clearly established. For example: FCA 33 Avenue President Wilson, Paris, France, Incoterms® 2020.

Delivery time in EXW conditions:

In case of using the Incoterms EXW, it specifies in the sales conditions the period of days in which the buyer must load in the seller's warehouse. The time of delivery under Incoterms EXW occurs when the seller makes the goods available to the buyer at his warehouse. Setting a maximum date exempts the seller from the risk of deterioration of the goods if the buyer has been excessively late in coming to collect them from his warehouse.

FOB in air?

The Incoterms FOB as we know is exclusive for the maritime transport. Therefore, the right thing to do in the case of air shipments is to use "FCA Merchandise Loaded on Board Aircraft"

Delivery and risk in Incoterms group C:

Group C Incoterms (CIF, CFR, CIP, CPT) are contracts for shipment, not contracts for arrival or delivery at destination. Delivery occurs at origin, as with Group F Incoterms. The responsibility for the goods during the main transport is the buyer's, so it is the buyer who has the risk of the goods from the moment of delivery at origin to destination.

Specify time of delivery in Incoterms CPT/CIP:

In the CPT/CIP Incoterms the seller delivers the goods to the main carrier at an agreed place of delivery and pays the freight to the agreed place of destination. The transfer of risk occurs after loading at origin, even if the seller pays for carriage to an agreed point at destination. For this reason, it is advisable to specify the time of delivery at origin in order to delimit risk responsibilities of the goods. For example: CIP Veracruz, Calle del Coronel 32 (delivery at Plaza Mayor 10, Cuenca, Spain). Incoterms® 2020.

Insurance of goods in Incoterms CIP/CIF:

For sales with CIF or CIP terms, the insurance coverage and its geographical and temporal scope must be specified, i.e. where and when it begins and ends. In this case, specific insurance must be taken out for each trip and 110% of the CIF value, and global policies and civil liability insurance for means of transport are not valid. According to the recent publication of Incoterms 2020, it is a mandatory condition to contract minimum insurance with IC Clause C for CIF term while IC Clause A for CIP term.

Reservation of title clause in contracts:

Since Incoterms do not reflect the transfer of ownership of the goods, please remember to include the retention of title clause in contracts, purchase orders or commercial invoices.

For example: "Buyer Company X indicated on this invoice will acquire ownership of the goods when it has demonstrated full payment.

Printed by Books on Demand GmbH, Norderstedt / Germany